Tomorrow's World

LIVING IN THE FUTURE

Mark Lambert

Tomorrow's World

First published in 1985 by Wayland (Publishers) Limited
49 Lansdowne Place, Hove, East Sussex BN3 1HF, England

© Copyright 1985 Wayland (Publishers) Limited

British Library Cataloguing in Publication Data
Lambert, Mark, 1946–
Living in the future. – (Tomorrow's world)
1. Technology – Juvenile literature
I. Title   II. Series
600   T48

ISBN 0–85078–581–2

Phototypeset by Kalligraphics Ltd., Redhill, Surrey
Printed in Italy by G. Canale & C.S.p.A., Turin
Bound in Great Britain at The Bath Press, Avon

Contents

Building tomorrow's homes

Ever since our distant ancestors began living in caves, shelter has been one of our most basic needs. Over the years, the style and comfort of homes gradually improved. Caves and tents made of skins were replaced by houses built of mud and straw. In turn these gave way to houses built of timber and bricks. Today a home is where people cook, eat, sleep and relax in privacy and comfort.

At present most houses are built using timber and bricks or concrete blocks.

A prefabricated section is carefully lowered into place. In system building prefabricated building parts are assembled on site.

Materials and construction

The basic style of the houses found in the Western world was established hundreds of years ago, and at the moment people still seem to prefer living in houses that have a 'traditional' appearance. Building materials have changed, but not all that much. Most houses are still built using bricks or concrete blocks and timber.

But future homes may be very different. Changes may occur for two important reasons. First, building houses by traditional methods is becoming very expensive. Second, present-day houses are very wasteful of energy.

One of the building materials that is becoming more and more expensive is timber and this may become scarce in the future. At the same time, the process of laying bricks and concrete blocks requires a lot of expensive labour. And

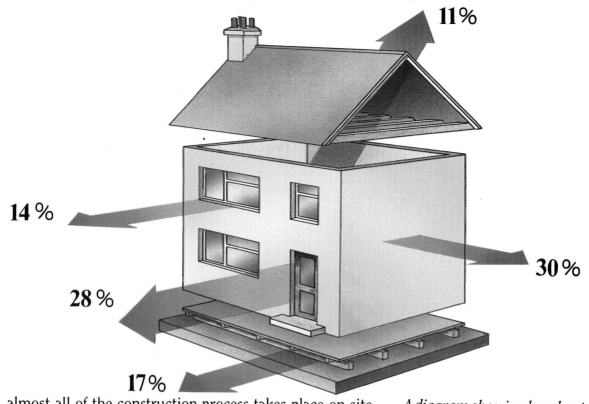

11%

14%

30%

28%

17%

almost all of the construction process takes place on site. There it is difficult to control the quality of the building, and poor weather can cause expensive delays.

These problems can be overcome by 'system building', in which houses are built from prefabricated sections – pre-made building parts that can be assembled on site. This is not a new process and in the past such buildings have proved unpopular. But this was because people built the wrong types of building or used materials that did not last very long. In the future, it should be possible to erect cheap, attractive, system-built houses, using materials that will last a long time and need very little maintenance.

Such houses will not all have to look the same. Using precision-engineered panels for outside and inside walls, it will be easy to change the size and design of houses to suit the needs of the people who want to live in them.

It will also be possible to build a house with movable wall panels. The owners will then be able to alter the design of their houses at any time they wish. Only the foundations need remain fixed. These, together with the mains services – electricity, gas and water – will probably still be laid in the traditional way.

A diagram showing how heat is lost from a typical home. A large proporation of the total heat loss passes through the walls, although draughts can also be the cause of a considerable amount of heat loss.

6

Saving energy

People who live in cold and temperate parts of the world use up a lot of energy in keeping their homes warm. Most present-day homes are very inefficient energy users. A typical home loses a lot of heat through its roof, and even more (over one-third of the total heat lost) through its walls. Energy is rapidly becoming more expensive and in the future some sources of energy may be difficult to obtain. So homes will have to be designed to reduce heat losses to a minimum.

Insulated walls reduce heat loss to a minimum.

The walls of an energy-saving house must be made of, or at least lined with, a material that is a good insulator. One method of building a heat-retaining wall is to build it in several layers, some of which are insulating layers, with air gaps in between. The outside of the house can be clad with any material to make it blend in attractively with its surroundings.

Roofs can be insulated in the same way as they are now, by using such materials as glass-fibre, mineral wool fibre and vermiculite chips. Floors can also be insulated using similar materials. Finally, an energy-saving house of the future must have well made and fitted doors and windows. They will almost certainly be double-glazed, although this is not as important as draught proofing – most present-day homes lose an enormous amount of heat through draughts. In fact, windows should remain closed nearly all the time while the heating is on. Ventilation can be provided by a system of fans and ducts, and any heat in the air being drawn off can be used to preheat the incoming air in a device called a heat exchanger.

Ideally, houses should be a hemisphere in shape – like an Eskimo's igloo – to keep the surface area through which heat can escape to a minimum. But we are not likely to see rows of highly-insulated hemispherical houses in the future. Such houses would not use very much energy, but they would not be able to make good use of the vast amounts of free energy that is available every time the sun shines. To use this, a house should have a large, south-facing wall, much of which is made of glass. On a sunny day in winter, the heat trapped by the 'greenhouse effect' can make a considerable contribution to heating the house. A

These system-built homes in New Mexico, U.S.A., were built with the idea of using as little mains energy as possible.

This south-facing building in Alabama, U.S.A., has a large array of solar panels used for heating and cooling.

system of reflective venetian blinds can be used to keep out unwanted heat during the summer and reduce heat loss at night. The windows must, of course, be double-glazed.

Town and country homes

It is clear that tomorrow's homes will be designed with saving energy in mind. But other factors will also have to be taken into account. The world's population is rising rapidly, and so it would seem that more high-density living accommodation will be needed in cities and towns. In the past, high-rise buildings were thought to be the answer. And some people still envisage such buildings being used in the future. But they are unpopular forms of housing and often deteriorate rapidly.

In places where the population is high, such as Hong Kong, high-rise buildings are at present the only way of providing enough homes for people.

The alternative – spreading houses over what is at present countryside – is equally undesirable. Countryside is needed for farming and recreation and should be preserved.

The solution to the problem is, therefore, likely to be a compromise. In towns and cities, high-density housing will probably be no more than three or four storeys high. Skillfully and imaginatively designed, such housing can use energy efficiently, with energy resources shared between homes. At the same time, they can be pleasant to live in and provide their occupants with the privacy they need.

In country areas, there will probably be more individual homes. Again, these will have to be energy-efficient and in some cases they will be autonomous, that is, they will have their own energy sources and be entirely independent of all mains services.

The countryside is needed for farming and recreation. So the space taken up by industry and housing must be kept to a minimum.

Automation in the home

A wide range of automatic machines can already be found in people's homes. There are simple ones, such as pop-up toasters, automatic kettles and immersion heaters. Others, such as washing machines, dishwashers, microwave ovens and electronic sewing machines, can be programmed to perform quite complicated tasks. In the future, homes will have these and probably other automatic machines. But it seems that there will be a limit to the amount of automation that can be successfully brought into people's homes.

Dishwashers and washing machines are very useful. But they leave quite a lot of work for people to do. And there are still many household chores, such as cleaning, ironing and mowing the lawn, for which there are no automatic

Automatic machines are common in today's homes.

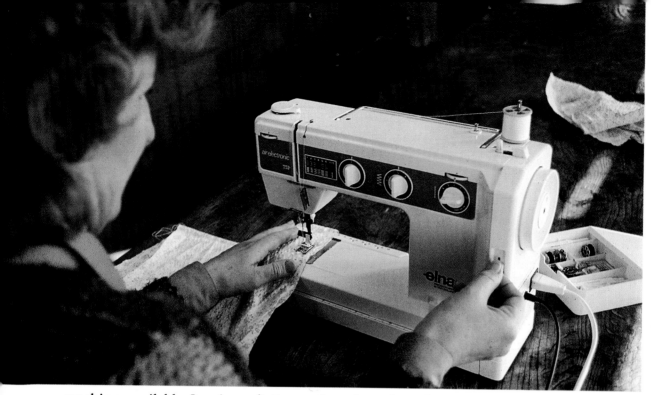

machines available. In science fiction such work, and much more besides, is done by robots. And, as industrial robots appear in ever-increasing numbers in factories, the prospect of domestic robots seems to get nearer and nearer. In fact, there are already some very simple 'domestic' robots.

But although the idea of having robots to do our cleaning, cooking and washing for us seems like an attractive one, would such robots be, in reality, practical or even desirable? The tasks that they would be required to do are actually very complicated, so programming such robots would be difficult. For example, a cleaning robot would have to know that the jigsaw puzzle you are in the middle of doing is not rubbish and so not sweep it up!

Even if the necessary programs can be devised, will robots be able to operate in our homes? Robots prefer well-ordered places that do not change. To a robot, most homes would seem chaotic, and even moving a chair might bring a cleaning robot to a complete standstill! Climbing stairs would also be a problem for most robots. In fact, we would probably have to thoroughly reorganize our homes to suit our robots!

This sewing machine has a small computer inside it and can be programmed to perform quite complicated tasks.

14

The so-called 'domestic robots' that have been developed do not seem to have much practical value. Most are little more than mobile microcomputers. However, such machines might be used as robot 'pets', which could, perhaps, perform simple fetching tasks and memorize essential information, such as shopping lists, telephone numbers and people's birthdays.

Computer-controlled homes

Automation in the home is more likely to be limited to the main systems that operate throughout the house. Computer-controlled heating and ventilation systems will be designed to make the most efficient use of the various forms of available energy at different times of day and night, and during different seasons. On a sunny day in winter, for example, the computer would switch over to solar heating. At other times the computer could decide to use gas or electricity to heat the home. When the occupants of the house go away for a time during the winter, the computer could monitor the temperature in all parts of the house and, if necessary, switch on the heating in some places to prevent frozen pipes.

The electrical system, too, could be monitored by the computer. It could give warning of faulty and potentially dangerous wiring and appliances. While the occupants of the house are away, the computer could be programmed to switch lights on and off at suitable times, in order to deter burglars.

This 'personal domestic robot' can be programmed to move around the house and carry things from room to room. It can also be programmed to speak.

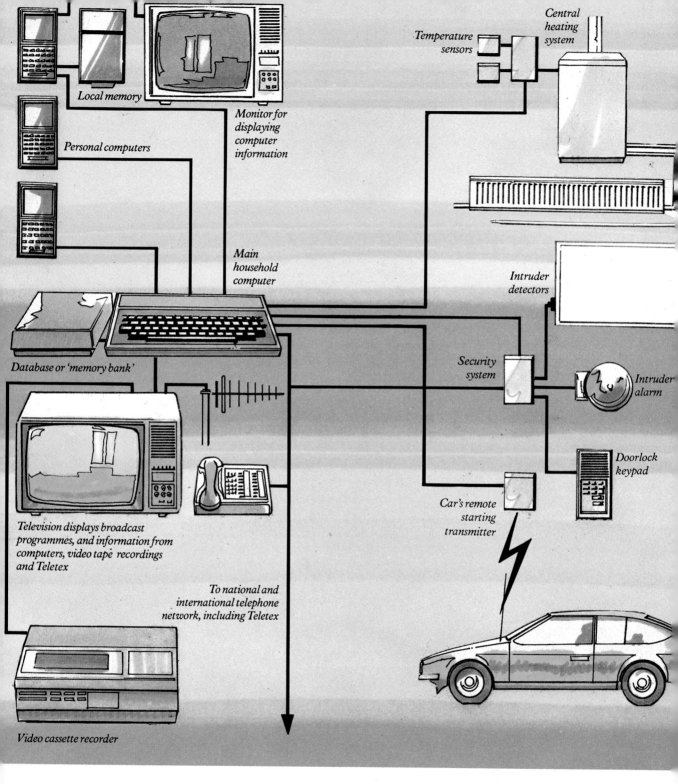

Local memory

Personal computers

Monitor for
displaying
computer
information

Main
household
computer

Database or 'memory bank'

Television displays broadcast
programmes, and information from
computers, video tape recordings
and Teletex

To national and
international telephone
network, including Teletex

Video cassette recorder

Temperature
sensors

Central
heating
system

Intruder
detectors

Security
system

Intruder
alarm

Doorlock
keypad

Car's remote
starting
transmitter

A computerized system like this one may be a common feature of tomorrow's homes.

Communications

It is now possible to talk to someone on the other side of the world at the press of a button.

Modern communications, together with modern transportation, have revolutionized our way of life. But now, in the age of electronics and digital computers, a new revolution is taking place. At present we have various methods of communication. But in the future these may become combined into a single system with many uses.

Below *The car telephone is just one of the many developments that have come from the revolution in communications.*

Telephones become electronic

The telephone, originally invented in 1876 by Alexander Graham Bell, has been improved and refined over the years. But the most dramatic changes are only now taking place. Until recently, all telephones worked using an analogue electrical system, and many still do. In this system, the speech picked up by the microphone in one handset is converted into a varying electrical signal, or audio wave. This passes down the wire and is turned back into speech by the speaker in the earpiece of the other handset. Calls are routed through telephone exchanges by mechanical switches.

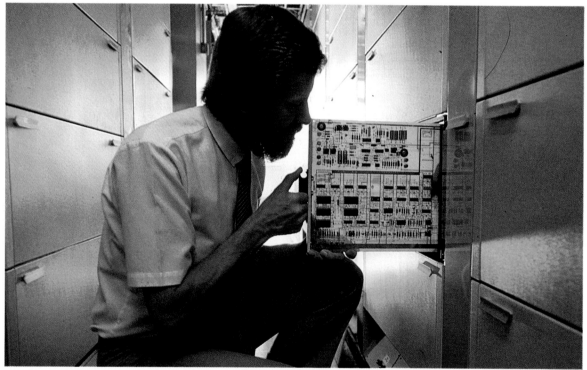

A modern electronic telephone, on the other hand, uses a different system. The telephone contains a silicon chip that can change the speech pattern into a stream of electrical pulses and back again into speech. The electrical pulses are called digital signals and form a code called binary code. Electronic telephones can work via mechanical exchanges, but increasingly, these are being replaced by fully electronic exchanges with no moving parts.

Today's exchanges are fully electronic. They have no moving parts and can work much faster than mechanical exchanges.

18

An optical fibre cable (left) can carry more telephone calls than a much larger electrical cable with copper wires.

A digital telephone system has several advantages. Electronic switching is quicker and more reliable than mechanical switching, and calls can therefore be routed much more rapidly. Unwanted noises and distortion of people's speech can be eliminated, and more calls can be sent down the same cable at any one time. Electronic telephones have memories that can store telephone numbers. And because they work using binary code – which is also the language of computers – they can be used for communicating with computers without the need for special devices called modems. Electronic telephone exchanges are controlled by their own computers. These control the routing of telephone calls and store information, such as the number and length of calls made by each user.

Other new developments are also improving the telephone systems of the world. For example, optical fibre cables are beginning to replace copper cables. The speech pattern, instead of being carried by electric current, is carried by laser light. Using laser light, just a few strands of optical fibre – each glass strand no thicker than a human hair – can be made to carry thousands of conversations. Optical fibre is much cheaper to produce than copper cable and telephone conversations transmitted by laser light are free from any electrical interference.

The increasing use of cordless telephones and radiophones means that you are no longer restricted to using a telephone in one place. Cordless telephones have handsets which allow you to make and receive calls a short distance away from a fixed base unit inside the house or building. The latest radiophone systems allow you to telephone or be telephoned regardless of where you are.

A cordless telephone can be used a short distance from a fixed base unit inside a home.

Telephones, televisions and computers

The fact that telephones and computers can now be linked easily is important. As more and more information is stored and processed by computers, it will become increasingly vital for people to be able to communicate with computers and for computers to communicate with each other. In fact, people can already use the telephone system to communicate with computers. In a Viewdata system (also known as Teletex), such as British Telecom's Prestel, subscribers can call up information on their television screens, simply by pressing buttons on a remote-control keyboard. The television is then automatically connected with the Prestel computer via the telephone.

The 'pages' of Viewdata information displayed on the screen are compiled by organizations, such as companies and government departments. They can call up their own pages and alter the information at any time, in order to

A computerized share dealing room in a bank. Links between telephones and computers are important to many organizations.

bring it up to date. At present, Viewdata systems are used mostly by businesses. Other people use the similar Teletext information systems, which is broadcast by the television companies, and so does not travel along telephone wires. But if the range of information that can be called up on Viewdata increases and it becomes cheaper to use, Viewdata will probably become commonplace in people's homes.

Teletext information is broadcast by television companies.

Home communications stations

If the revolution that is taking place in communications continues, it could lead to every home having its own multi-functional communication station. Instead of having separate telephone, television, video machine and micro-computer, all these will be combined into an integrated system that can be used in many different ways.

It will still be possible to telephone people in the normal way. But if the system is equipped with an additional tele-vision camera, it will become a 'videophone'. Users will be able to see each other, as well as speak to each other.

Telephone directories will be a thing of the past. To find a telephone number, it will only be necessary to call up the relevant Viewdata pages on the television screen.

Many offices could become obsolete as people work from their homes. They will use their communications stations to receive information from a central computer at the headquarters of their company. The information will be fed directly into the microcomputer, which can then deal with it according to the instructions of the person working at home. Any relevant documents, or pictures, can be transmitted by means of a 'facsimile' machine linked to the computer. Additional information might come from electronic libraries that could be called up on the system.

Aerials like this one are used to transmit and receive telephone calls by radio via satellites in space.

Right *With computers bringing vast amounts of information into every home, many people will be able to work without leaving the house.*

Left *Two-thirds of all intercontinental telephone calls are transmitted by satellites in space. These satellites also handle computer data, telex messages, video recordings and photocopies of documents and pictures.*

Shopping from home

The communications station will also be useful for shopping and personal business. For example, it should be possible to avoid time-consuming and tiring visits to the local supermarket. In order to buy goods, the shopper will merely call up the supermarket computer and ask for the goods that are available to be displayed. Goods can then be selected by punching in the appropriate code numbers. Paying for the goods will be done automatically. The supermarket computer will transmit the amount to be paid and the subscriber will then call up his or her bank and, using a personal identification number (PIN), instruct the bank computer to pay the supermarket. Meanwhile, the supermarket computer will send out instructions for the goods to be collected up at the warehouse, possibly by a robot.

25

Finally, they will be delivered to, or collected by, the customer.

It will be possible to do all kinds of banking transactions from home. The bank computer can be instructed to pay bills, transfer funds from one account to another, buy foreign currency and company shares, receive credits and send out statements. If the system is linked to the electricity, gas and water meters of the house, these can be read automatically and, with the customer's consent, the appropriate amount deducted from the account.

The system will not only be used for business purposes. A television screen will show all the usual television programmes. It may also be possible to call up a video library for particular programmes or films. At the same time it will be possible to 'download telesoftware' – receive computer programs – from Viewdata and Teletext companies. Some of these will be computer games, while others will be educational programs that will allow students to study at home.

An ordinary television set, with only a few modifications, can become the centre of a home information system: A = Live studio broadcast; B = Video tape recorded broadcast; C = Teletext information broadcast; D = Broadcast transmitter; E = Broadcast reception aerial; F = Home video cassette recorder; G = Viewdata information database; H = Telephone exchange; I = Voice telephone network; J = Household telephone; K = Modem; L = Personal computer.

Work and leisure

The revolution in electronics is leading to an ever greater number of robots and automated machines appearing in factories and offices. Increasing automation will inevitably lead to changes in people's working habits. But what will these changes be and how will people cope with them? There are various possibilities.

More work or shared work?

It is possible to compare the 'Electronic Revolution' of today with the Industrial Revolution that occurred in Britain during the 1700s and 1800s. Then, as now, machines replaced people in factories and, for a while, unemployment increased. But in time people did adapt to the situation and, in fact, found that new jobs were being created.

The modern electronics industry is also creating new jobs. In addition, more people are being employed in the service and information industries. But it remains to be seen whether there will be enough jobs for all those who need them.

If there are fewer jobs available than the number of people able to work, and unemployment on a large scale is to be avoided, then the amount of time which people work will have to change. Many people will have to work shorter hours so that jobs can be shared – two or more people being able to work at the same job at different times. In other words, the work that is available will be spread out so that all, or at least most, of the working population has a job that earns them a reasonable income. This situation will not happen easily. It will need action by governments and cooperation between people.

Robots assembling cars on a factory production line. Automated machines like these are leading to changes in people's working habits.

In the future there will be many exciting things to do and see.

28

Leisure activities

If people work shorter hours, they will have more leisure time, and this itself will help to create more jobs in a number of different industries. People will have more time to pursue hobbies, for which they will need equipment and materials. Many crafts that are currently disappearing may become common again. Traditional sports will continue and there may be new ones created, such as racing solar-powered light aircraft.

Travel will be easy and popular, and companies will be busy organizing tours to even the most remote parts of the world. It may be possible to take trips in a Space Shuttle Orbiter or in sun-powered balloons and airships. Submarines with large, transparent viewing saloons could give tourists a unique view of life under the sea.

At home, there will inevitably be a variety of electronic games to play and, perhaps, three-dimensional television to watch. But, as a relief from the gadgetry of the twenty-first century, people will probably still read books and play 'old-fashioned' games, such as cards and chess.

Energy for homes

We use a considerable amount of energy in our homes for cooking, heating and lighting. The most widely used form of energy is electricity – many homes use nothing else. Other commonly used sources of energy are natural gas, oil and coal. Electricity is popular because it is clean and 'instant'. But it has to be generated in power stations, mostly by burning coal or oil, or using the heat produced by nuclear reactors.

Coal and oil are 'fossil fuels', that is, they are the remains of animals and plants that lived millions of years ago. These fuel reserves took millions of years to form and we are using them up at a very rapid rate. The world's coal reserves may last another 300 years. But the known reserves of oil and natural gas will probably become exhausted in less than forty years.

At the Hoover Dam in Arizona, U.S.A., a hydroelectric power station uses the stored water to generate electricity.

Below *A coal-fired power station. Large coal-fired power stations waste a lot of heat. More efficient ways of using coal must be found.*

enerating electricity

here are ways in which the world can be made less depen-
ent on fossil fuels. Already there are a few hydroelectric
power stations, in which water descending a mountain
slope is used to turn turbines. These power generators,
which produce electricity.

In the Rance estuary in France, tidal power is used to
turn turbines, and in a number of countries, there are
geothermal power stations. Heat from deep underground
turns water to steam, which is then used at the surface to
produce electricity.

The solar furnace at Odeilo in France.

Attempts are also being made to produce power using the same process that produces the sun's energy – nuclear fusion. At present the extreme temperatures needed to make the reaction work are a problem. But if successful nuclear fusion power stations can be built, they will be far cleaner and safer than existing nuclear power stations.

The sun's energy is free and in order to make use of solar power on a large scale, huge solar furnaces have been built. At the solar furnaces at Odeilo in France, banks of mirrors track the sun and reflect its rays onto an enormous curved mirror. This focuses the rays onto a furnace, which can reach 3,000°C (5,432°F). Another idea is to build huge solar-power satellites. They would orbit the earth, collect energy using solar cells, and transmit it down to earth's surface in the form of microwaves. Scientists are also experimenting with devices for extracting useful power from waves and currents in the sea.

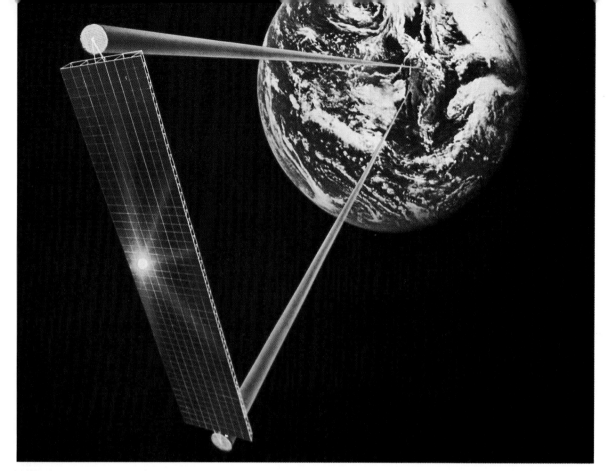

Other sources of energy

Individual houses or groups of houses may have their own sources of energy. Solar panels on a roof can collect enough heat to supply a domestic hot water system, particularly during the summer months. The sun's heat is collected by water that flows through the panels, and is then transferred to the domestic hot water and central heating system by means of a heat exchanger.

Unfortunately, in temperate countries, the sun does not shine very much at times when houses most need heating. One answer is to store heat during the warm summer months for use during cold winter periods. At present, the best method seems to be to store it in underground water tanks or in deep rock. In the future, there may be chemical methods of storing heat.

Another source of free energy is the wind. In places where wind speed is fairly constant and high, it is worthwhile installing a windmill. This can be used to drive a

Some people vizualize the development of huge solar-power satellites in space. They would beam energy down to earth in the form of microwaves.

34

generator to produce electricity, which can be stored in batteries. On a larger scale, a windmill can be combined with a hydroelectric scheme. The windmill is used to pump water uphill. When electricity is required, the water is released through turbines.

The heating system can be assisted by a device known as a heat pump, which turns large amounts of low-grade heat into small amounts of high-grade heat. It works in the same way as a refrigerator, in which heat is extracted from the air inside the fridge and given off by a radiator at the back. A heat pump can extract useful heat from the air, the ground, or better still, running water. Alternatively, it can be used to reclaim waste heat from the drains. A heat pump can be used in conjunction with a solar heating system. Solar power is used to produce warm water, which is then used by a heat pump to produce hot water.

A 'wind farm' in California, U.S.A. The wind's energy is collected by the windmills and converted by generators into electricity.

The houses in this energy-
efficient village of the future
have solar panels and south-
facing glass walls. Nearby are
a small coal-burning power
station and a windmill.

Household fuels

In the foreseeable future, coal will probably remain a useful and popular fuel for domestic heating. The best way of using coal is in medium-sized boilers that can supply heat to a number of homes at the same time. Coal-fired power stations and open domestic fires are very wasteful of heat.

Alternative fuels can be produced from waste materials. In some parts of the U.S.A., refuse is compressed into pellets which can be burned. And in one part of London, household cooking is done using a gas called methane supplied by the local sewage treatment works. Smaller communities can process domestic waste in a special container, or digester, to produce biogas. This contains 65–75 per cent methane, and can be used for cooking, heating and even lighting.

Finally, some people believe that the 'fuel of the future' is hydrogen. It certainly has several advantages. It burns at a high temperature and can be stored fairly easily. It contains more energy than petrol, weight for weight, and creates less pollution. However, the problem of producing hydrogen – by splitting water into hydrogen and oxygen – cheaply enough to make it worthwhile has yet to be solved.

Future transport

Automation and the availability of fuels are the two things that will most affect transport systems of the future. At present, most methods of transport depend either directly or indirectly on the petroleum industry. But in thirty years oil, and hence petrol and diesel fuel, may be in short supply. New kinds of fuel will have to be found.

An off-shore drilling platform. The known reserves of oil and gas will probably run out in less than forty years.

Busy roads and flyovers in Tokyo, Japan. Tomorrow's motor vehicles may have hydrogen-burning engines. These will not produce the pollutants produced by existing engines.

Fuels of the future

When the oil reserves run out, petrol may not immediately become a thing of the past. Coal, which will still be plentiful, can be refined into petrol, diesel oil, jet fuel and liquid petroleum gas – another fuel that can be used in motor vehicles – together with natural gas and other useful chemicals. In South Africa there are already two plants producing petrol from coal.

Another fuel that is already being used is ethanol, or ethyl alcohol. This is the alcohol found in alcoholic drinks, and it is produced by fermenting sugar and distilling the resulting liquid. Ethanol has been used as a fuel in racing cars for many years. Mixed with petrol it is known as gasohol. This fuel is used in Brazil, where sugar cane is grown in order to produce the ethanol.

Other food crops may be used to produce ethanol in the future. But the use of ethanol on a large scale may be limited to large tropical countries like Brazil. In temperate countries, it is not possible to grow sufficient plant material to produce fuel alcohol economically. And in densely populated countries, growing crops for fuel could lead to food shortages.

Methanol, or methyl alcohol, is chemically very similar to ethanol, and is equally as good as a fuel. It can be produced from coal, wood, sewage and other waste materials. At present, methanol is expensive to make, but

in the future cheaper ways of producing it may be discovered.

Hydrogen is also being considered as a fuel for tomorrow's cars. It burns very well in internal combustion engines, and only minor changes to the engines are needed. A hydrogen-burning engine does not produce the polluting chemicals emitted by petrol engines, but it does produce its own harmful pollutants unless water is injected into the engine cylinders.

Hydrogen can be supplied as a gas or as a liquid – at a temperature of below −253°C (−487°F). But, for use in cars, it is too dangerous in either of these forms, as it is highly flammable. However, there is a safe way of storing hydrogen. Some metal alloys can absorb vast amounts of hydrogen. If such an alloy is then heated, hydrogen is given off. So the 'fuel tank' of a hydrogen-powered car will probably be a container packed with granules of a hydrogen-absorbing metal alloy.

Modern cars on a factory production line. Energy considerations are not yet considered by manufacturers to be more important than comfort.

Future cars will use fuel much more economically than present-day cars. They will have streamlined shapes and efficient engines.

Tomorrow's cars

Whatever kind of fuel is used in the future, it is not likely to be cheap. So the design of future cars will reflect the need for fuel economy. Today's car engines turn only about a third of the fuel they use into useful work. Tomorrow's car engines will have to be much more efficient. Computers will control how fuel is used. Cars will also become much more streamlined as engineers continue to try and reduce drag – the resistance met by a car as it pushes through the air – to a minimum.

Tomorrow's cars may have improved piston engines. On the other hand, some manufacturers are working on gas turbine engines. These may be able to save up to a third of the fuel used by piston engines. Electric cars, too, are possible, although several problems will have to overcome. Batteries will have to be made less bulky and heavy, and the range and speed of electric cars will have to be improved.

An alternative idea is the hybrid car. In one experimental diesel-electric car, the wheels are turned by battery-powered electric motors. A diesel engine turns a generator to keep the batteries powered up. The advantage of the hybrid car is that its diesel engine runs at a constant speed whilst it is providing energy for the batteries. This is much more economical than running a diesel or petrol engine at varying speeds, as in a conventional car.

Tomorrow's trains

Speed is vital on the world's intercity railway networks, and modern trains are being designed with this and passenger comfort in mind. Trains such as the British APT (Advanced Passenger Train), the bullet-nosed Japanese *Hikari* ('lightning') trains, the French TGV *(Turbotrain à très grande vitesse)*, and the Russian ER 200 are being designed as complete, streamlined units. These are the kind of trains we can expect to see more of on major railway routes in the future, instead of the collection of miscellaneous coaches attached to locomotives that are commonplace today. The 'new' trains will be controlled increasingly by computers rather than people. The age of the fully automatic railway is approaching.

A bullet-nosed Hikari *train on the Shinkansen line between Tokyo and Osaka in Japan.*

Most modern high-speed trains are powered by electric motors or gas turbine engines. Steam is generally considered to be a relic of the past. But this may not be so. It is likely that a completely new design of steam locomotive will soon appear. It will use fuel much more economically than electric or diesel trains. A new design of boiler will allow the burning of coal to occur more efficiently, and without the production of smoke, cinders and sulphur dioxide gas. Nor will the locomotive need to stop to take on water, because its steam will not be released into the air. Instead it will be reclaimed by condensing it in huge air-cooled radiators.

Inner-city transport

Modern cities are becoming increasingly congested with cars and other vehicles. Mass transit systems do exist, but they are often inefficient and overcrowded. Future city transport systems will have to be designed to overcome these problems.

The most important part of a city's transport system will be a network of electric underground trains, similar to the underground system already found in some major cities. Existing networks use electric motors supplied from electrified rails. In the future, we may see trains without wheels. They will be suspended above the track by magnetic levitation (maglev for short), and propelled by 'linear induction motors' – a kind of electric motor. Such trains will

HELIPORT

CITY METRO

be swift and silent and they may well be completely automatic, operated by a central computer.

Above ground, transport will also be important. Semi-automatic buses could run in specially designed concrete trackways. There may be overhead monorail systems for transporting people between city centres and airports. And in the more distant future we may see moving walkways and robot taxis that can take people to exactly where they want to go completely automatically.

Some of the transport systems that may be found in a city of the future.

Glossary

Alloy A mixture of two or more metals.

Automation The process of introducing automatic and automated machines, including robots, into factories and homes.

Binary code The language used by computers. The language is represented electrically by pulses (1s) and no pulses (0s). Electronic switches in a computer turn on and off to produce the pulses.

Digital Concerned with numbers.

Facsimile A method of sending exact copies of pictures and documents by telegraph.

Greenhouse effect An effect occurring in greenhouses and buildings in which the heat from the sun passes through the glass or a window, warming the contents, the heat given out by the contents inside being trapped by the glass.

Heat exchanger A device for transferring heat from one fluid to another, separate fluid.

Liquified petroleum gas (LPG) One of the gases, such as butane or propane, produced from crude petroleum at a refinery. These gases are liquid when stored in containers under high pressure.

Magnetic levitation (maglev) A method of lifting an object off the ground using an arrangement of magnets and electromagnets.

Nuclear fission The spontaneous breakdown of the nucleus of a radioactive atom that produces energy and radiation.

Nuclear fusion The fusion, or union, of deuterium and tritium (two special forms of hydrogen) to form helium. The process can only occur at extremely high temperatures and pressures, but when it does occur vast amounts of energy are released. The process occurs in the sun.

Solar cell A device that converts light into electricity.

Solar panel A device that absorbs heat from the sun and transfers it to a liquid, usually water.

Teletext A system where information is broadcast over a television channel. Oracle and Ceefax are the national Teletext services in Britain.

Viewdata (Teletex) A computer system where information is sent along the telephone line and displayed on the television.

Further reading

If you would like to find out more about living in the future, you may like to read the following books:

Computers in Everyday Life by Ian Litterick and Chris Smithers (Wayland, 1983)

The Computerized Society by Steve Pizzey and Sheila Snowden (Wayland, 1985)

The Autonomous House by Brenda and Robert Vale (Thames and Hudson, 1975)

Information Revolution by Lynn Myring and Ian Graham (Usborne, 1983)

Transport on Earth by Neil Ardley (Franklin Watts, 1981)

The World of Tomorrow by Robin Kerrod (Longman, 1980)

Index

Acknowledgements

The publishers would like to thank all those who provided pictures on the following pages: British Telecommunications PLC 18, 19, 20; Bruce Coleman Limited 2–3, 7 (R. P. Carr), 23 (P. Davey), 25 (E. Chrichton); Camerapix-Hutchison 12 (M. Rock); Maltings Partnership 28–9, 36–7, 44–5; PHOTRI 9, 10, 24, 30, 34; REX Features *cover* (Danilo Boschung/Skyline Features), 12, 41; Science Photo Library 21 (P. Ryan); TOPHAM 13, 14, 17; Malcolm S. Walker 6; ZEFA 4 (G. Mabbs), 5 (H. Lutticke), 11, 27 (Bramaz), 31 (T. Ives), 33 (G. Kalt), 43.